BYGONE BATTLE

BYGONE BATTLE

Aylwin Guilmant

Phillimore

1983

Published by
PHILLIMORE & CO. LTD.
Shopwyke Hall, Chichester, Sussex

ISBN 0 85033 500 0

Printed and bound in Great Britain by
BILLING & SONS LIMITED
Worcester, England

LIST OF ILLUSTRATIONS

1. A detail from the Bayeux Tapestry
2. Map of the battle, 1066
3. Painting of the Gateway
4. Cattle Market, c.1920
5. View of Battle Church, drawn by
   J. Vidler
6. The monument of Sir Anthony Browne
7. Powdermill Pond
8. The Duchess of Cleveland
9. Yeomanry Camp
10. Ploughing on a farm
11. Working on the Crowhurst cutting
12. The Zion chapel
13. Cock and Hen Cottage
14. Map of Battle, 1616
15. The Norman Stone
16. Souvenir of the 'Normand' Ceremony
17. South-west view of Battle Abbey
18. View of the Abbey
19. Ruins of the Abbey dorter
20. A coach and four in front of the Abbey
21. South-west view of the Abbey
22. Lithograph of Abbey entrance
23. Remains of the cloisters
24. The Upper Terrace at the Abbey
25. The east front cloisters
26. Crypts under the dorter
27. Crypts under the dorter
28. The dorter
29. Ruins of Abbey altar
30. Bishop Odo's tomb
31. Battle Abbey School girl by a stew
    pond
32. Aerial view of Abbey
33. Isaac Ingall
34. The Abbey Library
35. The Abbey Drawing room
36. The Abbot's Hall
37. The Duke of Cleveland
38. The Duchess of Cleveland
39. Mr. David Potter
40. Gargoyles
41. Obverse side of Abbey Seal
42. Battle Abbey Sale Catalogue
43. Battle Abbey Sale Catalogue
44. Early drawing of St Mary the Virgin's
    church
45. The churchyard wall
46. Undated view of church
47. Sketch of the interior of the church

48. Section of church
49. Battle Abbey Girls studying art in
    the dorter
50. Ancient features found at Abbey
51. Ancient features found at Abbey
52. Fire at Battle Abbey School
53. Fire at Battle Abbey School
54. Air view of Ashburnham Place
55. Ashburnham Place
56. Staircase, Ashburnham Place
57. The King's garments
58. Bertram, 4th Earl of Ashburnham
59. Bertram, 4th Earl of Ashburnham
60. Six Ashburnham brothers
61. Normanhurst Court
62. Pompeian Room
63. A wartime scene at Normanhurst
64. Lady Idina Brassey
65. The Brassey family on their yacht
66. Menu card
67. Invitation card
68. Fire at Normanhurst Court
69. A parade of scouts
70. W. C. Till, Ironmongers
71. W. C. Till, Ironmongers
72. W. C. Till, Ironmongers
73. An old ledger
74. Mr. C. Turner's shop
75. The cycle shop
76. A railway van
77. Mr. Jack Bailey at work
78. The Old Blacksmith's forge
79. Interior of the forge
80. The King's Head
81. The spillway
82. The Powdermill and grounds
83. Powdermill Pond and Cottage
84. Mr. James Morgan
85. Runner stones
86. Tree felling
87. Demolition of the tanyard
88. Shoe shop
89. J. Holland's butchers shop
90. Mr. Slatter
91. Mr. and Mrs. Jenner in their car
92. Allwork's shop front
93. High Street
94. The post office
95. The post office
96. Oxen at Pepper-in-Eye Farm

97. Battle cricket ground
98. Loading milk
99. Milkman
100. Milklady
101. Langton House and the Green
102. High Street and Abbey
103. High Street
104. Abbey Green and High Street
105. High Street decorated for the Coronation
106. Abbey Green
107. Battle Brewery
108. The entrance to the Brewery
109. The Pilgrim's Rest
110. Entrance to Battle hospital
111. The Wellington Hotel
112. Mount Street
113. Barrow, the furniture makers
114. Upper Lake
115. Upper Lake
116. Lower Lake
117. House Sale Notice
118. Lake House
119. 'View of Standard'
120. Railway Bridge
121. Battle Station
122. Battle Station
123. Train leaving Battle Station
124. The Deanery
125. The Grammar School
126. The Police Station
127. The Superintendent of Police
128. Crowhurst Viaduct
129. Crowhurst Viaduct
130. Rocks Gate
131. Hastings to London Road
132. Country lane
133. Battle Mill
134. Three paintings by Grosse
135. Newbery's delivery van
136. Mr. H. Wheaton & son in their van
137. Mr. Percy Boxall

138. ⎫
139. ⎪
140. ⎬ The 1932 Battle Pageant
141. ⎪
142. ⎪
143. ⎭
144. Re-enactment of the Battle of Hastings
145. A 'meet' on the Abbey Green
146. A 'meet' on the Abbey Green
147. Two young riders
148. Mr. and Mrs. Jenner in their car
149. Registration certificate
150. Boxing Day Meet outside the Gatehouse
151. The Cycling Club
152. A 'meet' outside the Station Hotel
153. A well-known Battle bus
154. A well-known Battle bus
155. 'Peer's Homecoming'
156. The Fire Brigade
157. Mr. Raper
158. The Raper family
159. Old men sitting on a seat
160. Football team
161. Marbles Match
162. Prospecting for water
163. Outside the *George Hotel*
164. The Langton School
165. Battle Policemen
166. Mr. H. Metson
167. A peculiar address
168. Old people at the workhouse
169. Caroline Mathews
170. Mr. R. Rae and his Canadian Farm
171. Mrs. Rae at her stove
172. Battle Fair and Market
173. Battle Fair and Market
174. Bonfire Boys
175. Fancy costume
176. Front cover of Fireworks programme
177. Royal visit
178. Map showing town of Battle

This book is dedicated
to
the people of Battle, East Sussex

PREFACE

This peaceful Sussex town seems remote from scenes of conflict, yet it owes its foundation and its name to William the Conqueror's victory at the Battle of Hastings. The great Abbey he built to commemorate the event remains today the most famous sight in the town: yet the streets of the little town which grew up about its gates have many architectural and historical tales to tell of their own. It has always been an important market centre; for much of its history it was also a centre of the gunpowder manufacturing industry. Although some of the great country houses which dominated life in Battle in the past can no longer boast the same owners, it has given me particular pleasure to see how many present-day families can point to grandfathers or even great-grandfathers who, like them, were proud citizens of Battle. This book sets out to record in photographs the past life of this old town — a way of life vanished forever.

ACKNOWLEDGMENTS

I would like to thank the following for their permission to use certain of their photographs and other relevant material; also for the help of many people so willingly given: The Museum of Battle & District Historical Society, and in particular the late Miss Josanne Robinson, Mr. E. J. Tyler and Mr. K. Clarke, East Sussex County Library, particularly Mrs. C. Jacobs, Hastings Museum, and in particular Ms. Victoria Williams. My grateful thanks also to Mrs. Pamela Haines, the Bexhill Area Librarian for placing much useful information at my disposal. Also the following of Battle: Messrs. R. Day, D. Beaty-Pownall, R. Emeleus, D. Jenner, H. Newbery, A. E. Stevenson, J. Woodhams, R. White and J. Webb. I should like to thank Mr. D. J. A. Teall, headmaster of Battle Abbey School and Miss S. Mumford, a member of his staff, for their help. My thanks also to the following who, whilst not living in the town, are nevertheless interested in it: Revd. J. and Mrs. Bickersteth of Ashburnham Christian Trust, Ashburnham Place; Mrs. Mary Freeman; Mrs. Philippa Kent; Messrs. G. C. Bridger, Barry Funnell, D. Hale, D. Swaffer, Michael Phillips and P. A. Hodgkinson.

BIBLIOGRAPHY

Books

Armstrong, J. R.; *A History of Sussex* (3rd edition, 1974)
Behrens, Lilian Boys; *Battle Abbey under 39 Kings* (1937)
Brandon, Peter; *The Sussex Landscape* (2nd edition, 1977)
Brakspear, Sir Harold; *Battle Abbey: An Illustrated Historical Sketch* (undated)
Brent, Judith A.; *Catalogue of the Battle Abbey Estate Archives* (East Sussex County Council, 1973)
Cleveland, Duchess of; *History of Battle Abbey* (1877)
Garmonsway, G. N.; (editor and trans) *The Anglo-Saxon Chronicle* (1953)
Harper, Charles G; *The Hastings Road* (1906)
Hodge, Vere F.; *The Parish Church of St Mary the Virgin*, Battle (1953)
Historic Buildings in Eastern Sussex, no. 1 (Rape of Hastings Architectural Survey, 1977)
Hobsbawm, E. J., and Rudé, G.; *Captain Swing* (1969)
Horsfield, T. W.; *The History, Antiquities and Topography of the County of Sussex* (1835)
Lowerson, John; *A Short History of Sussex* (1980)
Lowerson, John, and Myerscough, J.; *Time to Spare in Victorian England* (1977)
Phillips, Michael; *1066: Origin of a Nation - the Story of Battle Abbey, Sussex* (2nd edition, 1981)
Searle, E; (editor and trans) *The Chronicle of Battle Abbey* (1980)
Searle, E; *Lordship and Community: Battle Abbey and its Banlieue, 1066-1538* (1974)
Victoria County History of Sussex, vol. 19
Messrs. Ward Lock & Co.'s *Illustrated Guide Books* for 1922-3 and 1924-5

Newspapers, Articles and Pamphlets

The Times, 1830
The Hastings & St Leonard's-on-Sea Observer, 1914 and 1915
The Argus, 1966
Sussex Express and County Herald, 1830 and 1836
The Sussex Agricultural Express, 1830
The Cresy Report, 1850

Battle Town & Abbey Walk (East Sussex County Council booklet)
Battle, 1066 AD (Guide produced by the Battle and District Historical Society and the Battle Civic Association)
The Norman Conquest (Pictorial Booklet)
St Mary the Virgin's Church, Battle (privately produced booklet)

EDITION OF 1910.

EASTERN OR RYE DIVISION   BATTLE UNION   BATTLE U.D.   BATTLE PH.

XLIII. S.E.

Philcox Shaw

Police Station

Drill Hall

Cattle Sale Yard

Upper Almonry

BATTLE

Battle Park

North Lodge

Northtrade Road

Lower Almonry

Cricket Ground

St. Mary's Church

Deanery

Mount Street

School

Battle Abbey

Guest House

Refectory

Church

St. Martin's Abbey
(Benedictine)
A.D. 1067

Gas Works

Goods Shed

Station

BATTLE HILL

Harold Terrace

Starr's Green

Horselodge Plantation

Methodist Chapel

Lodge

New Pond

Tannery

Lodge

Site of the

Battle of Hastings

A.D. 1066

Lane End Lane

600 Yds.

500

Telham Court

Saxon Wood

Nursery

Warren Wood

Fish Pond

Downbarn Farm

400

Tank

300

200

Farthing Pond

Powdermill Lake

Park Dale

Barn Wood

Rifle Range

Downbarn

mill Wood

mill Lane

Campfield House

Pumping Station
(Battle U.D. Council)

Target

Hammond's Wood

Malthouse Wood

Burnthouse Wood

197

Telham Cottage

Estrella
Spring

Telham Hill Farm

Telham

Kell Wood

Miller's Farm

Peppering's Eye
Spring

Woodcroft

Allen's Wood

Corner Wood

Lower Peppering Eye

Footway Wood

Stamble's Wood

Coal Wood

Forewood Pumping Station
(Hastings Corporation Water Works)

Fore Wood

Introduction

The Battle of Hastings and the Founding of the Abbey

MODERN ENGLISH HISTORY may be said to commence with the Battle of Hastings fought on 14 October 1066, between the forces of the Saxon King Harold, and those of Duke William of Normandy. It set England on a new course, the results of which are still with us today; and gave us the town we know as Battle. The three earliest descriptions of the battle agree in essence. In William of Poitiers' account the Normans took the initiative whilst the Saxons resisted 'as though rooted in the soil'. The *Anglo-Saxon Chronicle* described the outcome in a few brief words. 'King Harold was slain, and Leofwine his brother, and Earl Gurth his brother, and many good men.' The Bayeux Tapestry gives a good pictorial account. Another source, the *Carmen de Haestingae proelio,* or Song of the Battle of Hastings, which was written before 1070, is today thought to be unreliable and biased.

Harold recoit une flèche mortelle dans l'œil et succombe.

Harold gets an arrow in the eye and dies.

1. From the Bayeux Tapestry: Harold is struck in the eye.

Harold's army fought on foot, his house-carles armed with two-handed battle axes, but the Normans used cavalry as well as foot soldiers. The Saxon army commanded the high ground. The engagement lasted eight hours; it is estimated that some 14,000 men took part, and the total casualties are believed to be a few thousand. Victory was assured by two stratagems; one was a feigned retreat by the left wing of the Norman forces, and, secondly, they shot their arrows into the air, raining them down on the hapless Saxon army. The remnants of Harold's warriors sought refuge in flight with the victors in pursuit. Crossing the uneven and treacherous ground, many of the Normans perished in a deep ravine later known as 'Malfosse'. Various locations have been suggested for its site; it is possible that the name was corrupted by 1279 to 'Manfosse', as a piece of land called 'Wincestrecroft in Manfosse' was ceded to the abbey in that year.

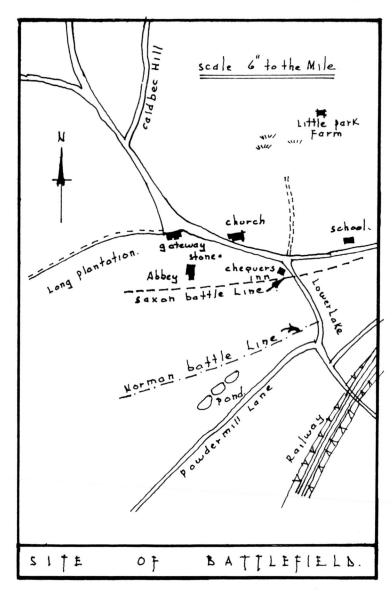

2. Site of the battlefield as shown in *A Short Guide to Battle* by Lewis H. Pyke. (*Reproduced by courtesy of the Battle & District Historical Society*)

The name Battle is derived from the French word for battle, 'bataille'. The town was known as 'Bellum' in the first royal charters, 'La Batailye' in the 11th century, 'Batayle' in the 14th century, 'Bataill' in the 15th century, 'Battell' in the 16th century, 'Battel' in the 17th and 18th centuries, and now 'Battle'; it was born out of military victory and a King's Vow. (See the *Victoria County History of Sussex,* Vol. 19, p. 97.)

The town of Battle stands on the site of Senlac Moor, scene of the Battle of Hastings. Battle Abbey, referred to as the 'Mynster' in 1094, was founded here in fulfilment of a sacred promise William made before the battle that he would erect an abbey for 'the salvation of you all, and especially of those who fall'. The site chosen was on a waterless ridge and highly unsuitable, but King William insisted that the high altar of the church should be on the spot where Harold was killed. The cost was to be borne by the king, and much of the stone used in the building of Battle Abbey came from Caen.

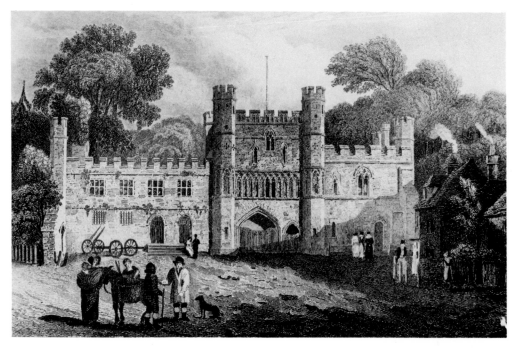

3. The Gateway, Battle Abbey, drawn by W. G. Moss, engraved by J. Gooden and published by G. Wooll of Hastings. Unfortunately it has been impossible to date this picture with any degree of accuracy.

Battle Abbey was a Benedictine house, richly endowed by the Crown and enjoying special privileges, as Searle tells us in *Lordship and Community: Battle Abbey and its Banlieu 1066–1538* (p. 23):

> The new foundation was granted for its immediate security and sustenance, a banlieu or 'leuga' as it is called in the abbey's records; all the lands lying within a league of the high altar, with sweeping immunities and with supreme jurisdiction over the land and men.

The monks were thus given resources of land and men to a distance of 1½ miles radius round the abbey in which the abbot had peculiar privileges, together with various manors in Sussex and other parts of the country.

Much of the abbey still stands, but little of the church. However, its plan is known through excavations. By 1076 it was sufficiently advanced for the second abbot to be blessed by the Bishop of Chichester, in front of the high altar. In 1094, the dedication of the church was performed by Anselm, the Archbishop of Canterbury, in the presence of William Rufus, son of William the Conqueror. While the monastic buildings were simple, the enormous guest-house suggests that Battle Abbey became for a time a considerable pilgrimage centre.

The Medieval Town

As a 'royal peculiar', the Abbey became one of the most influential establishments of its time. It was exempt from the jurisdiction of the Bishop; it possessed the rights of inquest, treasure trove, free warren, and the privilege of offering sanctuary. Its Abbots were mitred and had a seat in the governing councils which preceded Parliament; and they also possessed the prerogative of pardoning any criminal they might meet going to execution. (*Lordship and Community*, pp. 73–9.)

The town itself was originally built to house the craftsmen and labourers working on the great monastery and abbey of St Martin, and the geography of Battle enabled the monks to devise a town plan well-nigh perfect for a Benedictine house; isolated from mundane bustle, but with the advantages of all that a town could offer. (*Lordship and Community*, p. 73.)

The earliest account of Battle states that it consisted of 115 dwellings. It was divided into two areas; Claverham on the west side, and Sandlake on the east, each area having its own 'guildhall'. The guilds had a dual function, in that they oversaw trade and the quality of goods, as well as providing an opportunity for feast-days and other celebrations. Later in the town's history, the area between the market and the Abbey emerged as an entity on its own, called 'Middleborough' (see *Lordship and Community*, pp. 73–85). The town remained firmly under the control of the Abbey; it had no borough charter.

Much of the town must have fallen into disrepair after the Black Death of 1348 and 1361, and as one would expect, there is some evidence of 15th century rebuilding. Some of this, however, is hidden behind later facades. Battle must also have shared in the nationwide building boom of a period lasting at least a hundred years from 1550–1650, as many of the buildings date from this period.

In terms of population, Battle was basically an English market town, with only a handful of foreigners. Early in its history it was second only to Lewes in East Sussex, and the population is thought then to have been in the region of 1,500; following the Black Death it is estimated to have fallen to 1,000. A place of pilgrimage in the 12th century, it quickly became a tourist centre by the 15th century, which it still is today.

Markets and Fairs in Medieval Battle

If the Abbey was always the town's master, this had its advantages: 'From the beginning it had a weekly market held on Sundays granted by William I and free by the abbey's charters from all exaction save that of the abbey. In 1566 it was changed to a Thursday. Henry I granted the right to hold a 3-day fair in July, later was added a second fair held on the feast of St Martin in winter; as a result it became the market town of the region and well able to support its specialised workers, attracted by abbey patronage.' (*Lordship and Community,* pp. 80, 206.) Battle also became a local centre for cattle trading, and this brought a considerable income to the townsfolk, and also to the Abbey. Following the Dissolution the cattle market ceased until 1670, when it was re-established. The reason for this was said to be that 'Battle was 50 miles from London and the immediate towns had good accommodation for man and beast'.

4. The cattle market at the north end of the High Street was part of the Battle estate. In 1901 it covered 30 perches, and the annual rental was £10.

The medieval market must have presented a varied scene; for as Battle lay so near the coast, wine, salt, fish, and other goods were brought for sale from the Channel ports. Besides these goods, the Abbey archives record that cattle, poultry and other produce were regularly brought into the town from the Abbey manors in Kent and Sussex, whilst it had its own stew ponds for fish for the community's use. Battle was also important in that it was one of the collection centres for much of the local wool, which was later exported to the Continent. 'Many specialists of luxury articles and goods were attracted to Battle by virtue of the abbey and it was these products which gave the market its real advantage over potential rivals. It is thought that the decline of Battle market in the mid-15th century may have been occasioned by the growth of the new centres of trade in the High Street shops of whose activity each court roll is full.' (See *Lordship and Community,* pp. 352, 366.) Battle merchants would have found a steady market within the Abbey for many of their commodities.

Fairs at Battle

For many years there were annual fairs, although sometimes as in October 1666 they had to be cancelled. *The London Gazette* contained a proclamation stating 'That the infection being much spread about the town of Battle—though the inhabitants are free—yet to prevent its further spreading the fair usually kept on the 11th Nov. was directed not to be holden'. This announcement obviously related to an outbreak of the plague in the locality. The Whit Monday fair was abolished in 1875. The later fairs came to be known as the 'Pleasure and Cattle Fairs', the former, held on the Abbey Green, continued until 1938, and the latter until 1967.

The Founding of the Parish Church

The monks built a chapel for the use of townsfolk outside the Abbey wall, which came to be known as St Mary the Virgin's church. A priest under the direction of the Abbot served the parishioners, so the parish church came under the wing of the Abbey and benefited from its many privileges. The first small church was built between 1107-1124; the pillars in the nave are transitional Norman at the east end. The body of the existing church was built about 1230, enlarged in 1450 or thereabouts, and restored in the 19th century by Butterfield. The Deanery behind the church is an Elizabethan house, the building of which became necessary after the dissolution of the monastery, which had also housed the priest in charge of the parish. Originally the Dean, like the Abbot, was exempt from episcopal control and answerable only to the Crown. After the dissolution the Deanery lost its royal status, but nonetheless remained 'a peculiar', with the incumbent keeping his title of 'The Very Reverend, The Dean'.

5. An undated drawing of Battle church by J. Vidler. It will be noted that this lithograph was one of a series printed by W. Annan rather than the local printer and publisher W. Ticehurst. The date of this drawing is thought to be *c.*1820 in view of the unaltered elevation of the Deanery, seen in the background, as later in the 19th century the roof was raised in order to give further accommodation.

The Dissolution of Battle Abbey

For 471 years the Abbey continued to flourish, but with Henry VIII came the suppression of religious houses, and Battle shared in the general ruin. The Abbey was a rich prize, for it had an income in excess of many similar monasteries, and was, indeed, one of the wealthiest houses in England. The Abbot was accused of 'unnatural crimes', and in 1539 the king granted to Sir Anthony Browne, Standard Bearer of England and Master of the Horse, the house and site of the monastery of Battle. The Abbot and the remaining 16 brethren were dismissed on pensions. The 'plate and jewels' were reserved for the king, whilst 'the furniture and goods' were sold for only a small profit; it is thought that Abbot Hamond, the last of his line, had deliberately allowed the house to become run down.

Sir Anthony Browne was a devout Catholic, but despite this the monks regarded the Abbey's destruction and their expulsion as sacrilege. Legend has it that one of the monks put a curse on the family, proclaiming that they would perish by fire or water. When the family left Battle and went to live at Cowdray, in West Sussex, the curse seemed to begin to take effect! Henry VIII had made Sir Anthony guardian to his young daughter, Princess Elizabeth, and, following the king's death, it was thought she would be brought to Battle to live. With this in mind Sir Anthony began to build a great wing to the house, on the site of the Abbey guest-house, but he died before it was finished. His manor house, completed by his son, the first Viscount Montague, is still known as 'Princess Elizabeth's Lodging'. Through the centuries it fell into disrepair, and all that remain today are the two watch towers.

The Monument of S⁻ ANTHONY BROWN Kn⁻ of the Garter.

6. This drawing depicts the monument of Sir Anthony Browne and was published in 1777. It also shows the tomb of Alice, his wife. The fine tomb is in alabaster, elaborately carved and originally richly gilded and painted. The recumbent figure of the first lay owner of the abbey shows him clad in armour of the Tudor period and wearing the insignia of the Order of the Garter. The tomb was removed from its original site in the church on the orders of the Duke of Cleveland in the last century.

Crafts and Industries

1. *Clockmaking.*—Many of the early specialised crafts were due to Abbey patronage. Battle Abbey did not possess an elaborate astronomical clock, but there is a record of 'repair to the clock in the cubiculo of the sacristy in 1512, which cost 20 pence'. It is thought that this must have been a small clock of the type known nowadays as a 'monastic alarm'. (See E. J. Tyler, 'The Clockmakers of Battle', reprinted from *Antiquarian Horology,* 1978, p. 39.) The first record of the making of a clock in Battle was in 1656, when Thomas Punnett supplied a new clock for the church. During a period of nearly three hundred years 20 clockmakers lived and worked in the town, some of them of considerable eminence, but by the end of the 19th century very little in the way of manufacture was being carried out.

2. *Gunpowder Manufacture.*—The Weald of Sussex was the centre of the iron-making industry, and many of the rich ironmasters may have lived in the town of Battle. Pyke House, dating from 1569, was the residence of an iron finer. When the iron industry in the south ceased, Battle developed an alternative to it—the making of gunpowder, said to have been the finest in Europe. At Peppering-eye in 1676 four parcels of brook-land were let to John Hammond, with permission to erect a powder mill. Eventually Park Mill—now Powdermill House—became the chief of the mills in Battle. Battle was the exception to the general rule that only 40lbs. of powder was allowed to be made at one time under one pair of stones, and this may have been a contributory factor to the many explosions which occurred locally. The manufacture of powder lasted through the Napoleonic and Crimean Wars until 1874, when the Duke of Cleveland refused to renew the licences of the mills. Prior to 1627 a mill had been suppressed for the making of unauthorised powder at Battle, but little is known of this.

7. Photograph of the 12-acre Powdermill Pond at Battle.

3. *Brewing.*—Battle had its own brewery and it is believed that certain of their bottles were produced in the area. In the main the beer was distributed fairly locally. All these local enterprises gave employment during the hard years of the later agricultural depression.

Unlike many other similar market towns, the occupations of the inhabitants of Battle have been well documented, especially during that period in which the Abbey flourished. As early as *c.* 1110 Battle burgesses are listed together with their calling, while in the 15th century, Agnes Petyt was so regularly presented for being a 'pronuba' and for keeping a 'domus suspecta' that the subsequent small amercement or fine was evidently more a licence fee than a disincentive. (See *Lordship and Community,* p. 409.) Other inhabitants throughout the course of history have been more law-abiding!

4. *Leather Working.*—Another local industry was tanning. Hides were brought in and 'finished' at Battle Tannery. As early as the 14th century the Abbey records show a tannery was in existence. At one time, the number of tanners in Sussex stood at a constant figure of 135, but by 1900 this had fallen to eighty-five. Shoemaking (an offshoot from the tannery, but entirely independent) flourished, and hand-made shoes were a local speciality.

The Abbey, 17th–19th Centuries

During the Civil War, the royalist Montagues 'lost' 300 acres of Battle Great Park, and the coming of the Restoration hardly improved their fortunes. The fifth Viscount, a supporter of the Catholic James II, pulled down the Abbey kitchens and sold the materials. Much of the stone was used in the building of the *Bull* inn (now the *Nonsuch* hotel), in 1688. The stone was purchased at four shillings (20p) for a cartload.

In 1719 Sir Thomas Webster bought Battle Abbey and its estates from the sixth Viscount. He was a man of great wealth and had considerable property in London. At the same time, he purchased Bodiam Castle and the Abbey at Robertsbridge. His son, Sir Whistler Webster, reorganised the estate, but the property continued to decline during the 18th century. His grandson, Sir Godfrey (born 1798), was reputed to have spent huge sums renovating the property, but he was a notorious gambler and by 1825 he was ruined. He was forced to sell Bodiam Castle, Robertsbridge Abbey, £90,000 worth of timber, and also the unique collection of Battle Abbey deeds and documents. He received a miserable price for these muniments, which are now housed in the Huntington Library, California. In 1858 Sir Augustus Webster, the seventh baronet, sold the property to Sir Harry Vane (later Duke of Cleveland). The reign of his Duchess is still remembered; she took a great interest in the Abbey and the estate, and among other books wrote *The History of Battle,* published in 1877. It was the Clevelands who excavated Harold's Chapel, and did much to 'rediscover the Abbey'.

Following the death of the Duchess of Cleveland in 1901, Sir Augustus Webster, the eighth baronet, bought back the abbey for his family and it remained in their hands until 1976 when it was taken over by the Department of the Environment. For the past 60 years the buildings known as 'Battle Abbey School' have been let to a school for girls aged from 9–19 years.

8. The Duchess of Cleveland lived at Battle Abbey in the latter half of the 19th century. This photograph shows her with her famous white Borzoi and donkey chaise by her front door, *c.*1900. She persuaded the Duke to open the grounds to the general public. However, the visitors were more interested in making merry and the Duchess complained bitterly of the noise and litter. In her youth the Duchess had been strikingly beautiful, but a contemporary described her as 'agreeable & on the whole kind, but could be intolerant and sarcastic!'

Battle's Military Tradition

Battle has maintained a long military tradition which may be said to have begun, but not ended, in 1066. Battle was considered to be of sufficient importance to warrant garrisons being stationed there during the 18th and 19th centuries. During the invasion scares of the Napoleonic wars, a first reserve battalion was quartered in Battle. A barracks was built for the soldiers on the east side of the Whatlington Road, of which only Barrack Cottage remains. The site was chosen for these quarters because 'there was a sufficient quantity of water, to constantly supply two covered reservoirs, whence the inhabitants fetch it, when their wells fail'; the parade ground was on the Levels. Contemporary reports state that life at Battle was very gay, with dances for the officers at the 'Assembly Room' in the *George* hotel. Prince William of Gloucester came to the town in 1798, from Hastings, where he had been reviewing other troops gathered to oppose the expected invasion.

Like the early crusaders, whose small crosses decorate a pillar behind the Dean's stall in the parish church, Battle men have fought and fallen in the wars of this century, whilst the town itself suffered from enemy bombing, which damaged part of the Abbey gateway. During World War II, Canadian troops were stationed at Battle Abbey, whilst at nearby Normanhurst Court prisoners-of-war were housed.

9. Yeomanry Camp at North Trade Road, Battle, pre the 1914 War.

Nineteenth-Century Battle

1. *Agriculture.* —A guide book of the last 60 years described the town thus:

> It is a market town of about 3,000 inhabitants, but in spite of its sanguinary name, the population is mostly given over to the peaceful pursuit of agriculture. (Ward Lock and Co., *Illustrated Guide Books, Bexhill and East Sussex*, 1924, p. 75.)

In the early 19th century the town's dependence on agriculture had led to it suffering hardship.

In the agricultural depression after the Napoleonic wars, William Cobbett, the agitator, was said to have 'much excited the feelings of the paupers' when he lectured at Battle, and letters were written to the *Times* newspaper in this respect. This was not the case, as about a third of Cobbett's audience at Battle were in smock frocks, thus denoting their farming status. Despite Battle being one of the centres of the radical agitation in the south-east, outbreaks of arson were relatively rare, and usually directed at those out of sympathy with the rioters. One case of arson occurred at Course Barn farm on the Battle Abbey estate. Sir Godfrey Webster was known to be unsympathetic towards the labourers.

> Two Battle labourers, a man named Bushby and Thomas Goodwin, a cooper, were sentenced to death for arson. The authorities made efforts to implicate Cobbett in the rising and Goodwin signed a statement blaming Cobbett's lectures for causing it. He was pardoned and bustled from the country, but Bushby was hanged. The revolutionary was tried but acquitted due to the jury disagreeing, and the proceedings developed into a trial of the government, rather than of Cobbett. (Michael Phillips, *1066 Origin of a Nation—the story of Battle, Sussex.* 2nd edn., 1981, p. 45.)

Many of the outbreaks were directed against the overseers; a system for giving poor relief in return for work on farms under overseers was taken advantage of by unscrupulous farmers, which caused the poor rate to rise. In Battle, poor relief rose from £1,705 in 1803 to £4,000 in 1821. During rioting in the area one of the overseers was put in a dung cart and paraded through the street. Sir Godfrey Webster had 20 of the men arrested out of a crowd of 500 persons, but a sympathetic magistrate passed mild sentences, for which he was later officially censured.

> A Sussex landowner wrote to Sir Robert Peel that a message had been sent from the labourers assembled at Battle to those assembled at Sedlescombe (three miles east of Battle) and to the labourers in other adjoining parishes inviting them to join in organising a force for resisting the military which had just come down to Battle. (E. J. Hobsbawn and George Rudé, *Captain Swing*, 1969, p. 227.)

It was felt that the arrival of a single troop of the 5th Dragoons stationed at Battle tended to escalate the disturbances.

During this unsettled period of history Mechanics' Institutes were founded throughout the country:

> the original concept was for the poorer classes to set up improving, mutuality clubs of their own, although usually under suitable guidance. (John Lowerson and J. Myerscough, *Time to Spare in Victorian England*, Hassocks 1977, p. 102.)

> The Battel (*sic*) Institute came into being at an inauspicious moment when the town was suffering from severe agricultural depression and the bulk of its labourers were barely able to feed themself, let alone join a club for the literary minded (*op cit.*, p. 102).

10. Battle market served many of the surrounding farms, who sold their cattle there. This picture is typical of a scene which took place every springtime—note the three horses are walking abreast. The soil on many of the farms was heavy, but through the centuries the farmers continued to use oxen, since despite the fact that they required a far larger area to turn, they were more economical in that at the end of their working days their flesh and hide could be utilised. This picture was taken *c*.1890.

During 1831 many labourers of Battle were out of work for four months in the year, and from 30 to 80 persons for the other eight months. Poor Law relief paid amounted to over £2,000. The prevalent wage of an agricultural worker at this time was 12s. per week (60 pence), and few women were employed except for the occasional harvesting or weeding. The Mechanics' Institute tended to be used by the more well-to-do tradesmen rather than the labouring classes, who were unable to pay the moderate subscription of 1s. 6d. (7½ pence) a quarter.

2. *Transport.*—Due to its geographical position, Battle had rapidly developed as a centre of communications. As early as the 16th century Battle was served by post horse from Rye, and by 1800 it had become a 'Post Town', serving Bexhill and Sedlescombe. Mail coaches passed through the town *en route* to London and Hastings, and guide books of the period mention vehicles running from the *Swan* inn, Hastings, to the *George* inn at Battle, a distance of eight miles. *Cary's Itinerary,* a guide for travellers, written in 1821, shows the spelling as 'Battel', whereas a few years later *Paterson's Roads* of 1829 gives the modern version. In 1884 letters were postmarked at Battle with the number 54, and most types of business were transacted at Battle post office from this date.

3. *The Growth of New Industries.*—With the coming of the railway to Battle in 1852, conditions improved; many of the population now sought work in the expanding seaside resorts which were now accessible to them. Throughout the latter part of the 19th century the population continued to fall, and for those left the opportunities for employment became greater, with the opening of the nearby gypsum mines at Mountfield, and the growth of local industries in the town itself.

11. Working on the cutting, Crowhurst to Bexhill Railway, *c.*1900. The line passed through Crowhurst from Battle to Hastings and was opened early in 1852.

The countryside surrounding Battle became market gardens and orchards, much of this produce being sent to London and the coastal resorts. Newbery Jam factory came into operation at this time; later in its history it developed its sweet industry, one of the favourites being coloured 'fairings' made primarily for sale at Battle Fair.

During the last century Battle prospered as a market town. The increased trade was in specialist and luxury goods not obtainable in the surrounding villages. Sadly the small industries of the last century no longer function; today Battle brewery and the Newbery factory stand idle, the cattle market is no longer an important part in bringing revenue to the town, while the tannery was demolished within living memory.

4. *The Improvement of Living Conditions.*—In 1848, a Public Health Act (known as the Health of Towns Act) came into being; this was a 'permissive' rather than a 'mandatory' Act, which allowed enquiries to be made into the state of public health in any town, should a given number of the inhabitants request this to be done. At this time Battle was suffering from an inadequate water supply, which resulted in poor drainage. The two main sources were on Caldbec Hill, and at Loose Farm, where there was a pipe running to Rose Green (now called Starrs Green). Much of this supply came through seepage, with few actual pipes laid. Coupled with a high population density, the poor drainage resulted in ill health in the town; at this time the Battle death rate was noticeably higher than the average for the county. The Parish Vestry—the local authority of the time—requested an independent enquiry into the sanitary condition of the town; in 1850 a petition, signed by 50 of the most respectable and wealthy townspeople was sent to the General Board of Health. The outcome was that the Superintending Inspector, Edward Cresy, was appointed to investigate the situation and draw up a report.

The parish of Battle contained 7,880 acres of land, and it was estimated that there were 10 miles of road. Overpopulation led to an average number of six persons per house and 'there was no provision for the removal of any offensive or noxious refuse from the houses and gardens of the poorer houses, and there was no evidence that the streets or foot pavements were regularly swept, cleansed, or watered. Typhoid and other maladies had arisen in consequence of putrescent matters being retained too close to dwellings, from a want of a proper supply of wholesome water, and through lack of ventilation in some of the overcrowded habitations' (*The Cresy Report*, pp. 4–6).

Mr. Cresy held his first inquiry at the *George* inn in June 1850, and heard evidence from many of the townspeople. One inhabitant favoured the existing state of affairs, declaring that 'she had never experienced any smell and that the value of the sullage was considerable and she would be sorry to lose it'. This 'sullage' probably accounts for the better soil to be found in the High Street gardens, compared with others elsewhere in the town.

Mr Cresy recommended that a Local Board consisting of nine properly qualified persons, chosen from those who were rated at above £20 per annum, should be established. He also recommended sewers be built, and the owners of all cesspools should fill them in, and these houses should be connected to the main sewers. One general slaughter house should be established for the use of the butchers of the town (previously there had been seven). Reservoirs should be constructed, and a piece of land provided for the interment of the dead, the churchyard having become grossly overcrowded. It was this report that subsequently led to the formation of the Battle Board of Health in 1852, later in its history (in 1884) to become Battle Urban District Council.

5. *Nonconformity in Battle.*—Whilst Battle, like many Sussex towns, has not been remarkable for that radical Nonconformity which has influenced life in the more industrial north, the first of the chapels to be built belonged to the Unitarian movement. Erected in 1789 in Mount Street, it ceased to be used for worship before the Second World War, and in 1958 was demolished. The Zion chapel dates from the 19th century, likewise the Methodist, Wesleyan and Baptist. Only the Unitarian chapel had a place for interment, which was the front court adjoining the road.

12. The Zion chapel, which is almost next door to the Roman Catholic chapel, was built in 1820 and is in complete contrast to the style of the surrounding buildings.

Battle Today

Battle town as we see it today still preserves the typical layout of a medieval ridge town, but additional dwellings to house the rise in population during the 19th century were built on back gardens and disused inn yards. The additional newer properties have mainly been built during the 1930s, in particular along the approach roads. For most visitors to Battle, the Abbey is the main attraction, and the historical interest of the town itself may often be overlooked. However, a closer look will reveal the hidden charm of many of its old buildings, mainly 18th and 19th century, which have been largely refaced in deference to prevailing Georgian and early Victorian taste, and this, with the 20th century overtones, gives us the general appearance of the town today. The unique circumstances of Battle's foundation means that its story is more than that of a small Sussex town—it is part of the history of England.

SOME ASPECTS OF THE ARCHITECTURE OF BATTLE

The architecture of Battle is a medley of styles, and an inhabitant from any earlier century would have little difficulty in recognising the town he knew. In many instances one can see good examples of both Medieval and Georgian architecture with modern shop fronts superimposed on these facades.

The houses in general bear the mark of great antiquity, many being constructed of oak timber, originally without any metal fixing to avoid corrosion. The spaces between the framing were filled in with hard-packed loam on laths and wattle with a thin coating of plaster on the face which was only applied as ornamental covering. Internally, many of the houses had a large central fireplace with perhaps as many as four stacks; this served both for ventilation, and as a primitive form of central heating, in that the fires could be kept alight all night. The hearths were exceptionally large, often as long as eight feet and the width half that dimension.

Battle is rich in excellent examples of fine architecture; certain of the properties have been cited as first-class specimens of town houses of the period. Styles vary from half-timbered and stucco buildings, to those clad in 'mathematical' tiles. Other distinguishing features are Doric columns or pilasters (in several versions), jetty or overhanging first floors, corbelled brickwork, and elaborate canopies. Internally at least one building is known to possess a 'dragon' beam.

For those visitors interested in this particular aspect of Battle, two extremely good booklets on the subject have been issued, one an illustrated version entitled *Battle Town and Abbey Walk*, published by the East Sussex County Council, and the other a most informative leaflet called *Battle 1066 A.D.*, produced and published jointly by the Battle and District Historical Society, and the Battle Civic Association.

13. Lower Lake, 1875, going towards Hastings. Note the fall of the road is far greater than it appears to be today. On the left may be seen the cottages known as 'The Cock and Hen', because of their topiary.

From a map of Sussex by John Norden, augmented by John Speede.
a 1616 d.

14. An early map of East Sussex. It is interesting to see that Battle is mentioned but not the Abbey, whilst the Abbey at Robertsbridge to the north is marked, as 'Rotherbridge Abby'.

15. The Norman Stone, Battle Abbey.

16. Dedication of the 'Norman Stone' on 20 August 1903. This stone, erected by the 'Souvenir Normand' in commemoration of the Battle of Hastings, still stands on the spot where King Harold fell. Owner of Battle Abbey at the time of this ceremony, is the fourth gentleman on the right-hand side of the picture.

Battle Abbey

17. South West view of Battle Abbey in 1637 from a lithograph by W. Annan. It will be seen that the guest house with the twin towers is intact, while all that remains today of this great building are the two towers standing as sentinels to the past.

18. View of Battle Abbey, showing also part of the town. c.1810

19. This shows a view of the dorter dated 1807, and was painted by James Rouse, a drawing master of Fulham.

20. A coach and four drawn up in front of the Gateway, Battle Abbey early this century. Behind the crenellated wing on the left of the Gateway is a precinct wall adjoining it, and along this wall are steps and a ledge which would have enabled the Abbey watchman to do his rounds. The east wing was used as the court room of the Manor until the 18th century, and as a market hall during the same century.

21. West view of Battle Abbey drawn by J. Vidler.

22. A lithograph of the entrance to Battle Abbey. c.1800.

23. The remains of the cloisters, Battle Abbey. c.1830.

24. This photograph shows the upper terrace, all that remains of the 16th century house.

25.   A photograph of the east front of the cloisters, Battle Abbey.

26.   Lying to the south of the mansion at Battle Abbey is the famous range of monastic
buildings comprising the unroofed dorter (the sleeping place) and the three rooms below
it. In addition to the main staircase by which the monks ascended to the dorter, there was
a small private staircase for the Prior's sole use. The most northerly of the three rooms
below the dorter was the "Warming Room"; as the name denotes it was heated, by braziers.
The ribbed roof, unadorned, but very attractive, was supported by Purbeck marble pillars.
Next is a small room, which may have been a scriptorium when the cloisters ceased to be
used for that purpose. The function of the lowest chamber, which, owing to the slope of
the ground, is the highest pitched, is uncertain but it may have been a novices' room.

27. The vaulting of these crypts is the supreme achievement of the Gothic architects' and masons' skill and ingenuity, and this is a fine example of the period. The floor at one time may have been of marble.

28. The dorter or dormitory, on the east side of the Great Cloister Garth, was above the crypts and arranged to accommodate about 80 monks.

29. For nearly three centuries all traces of the splendid 'minster' erected by the Conqueror were effaced and it was not until 1817 that Sir Godfrey Webster cleared the overlying rubbish. He found the fragments of the high altar, standing at the end of the end of the chancel in front of three converging chapels, the ground plan of which has been likened to a crown. William erected the High Altar on the spot where Harold fell. Lying behind the altar was a processional path.

30. A photograph purporting to show Bishop Odo's Tomb at Battle Abbey. He was considered to be a leader in the spiritual life of his day and an author of some merit. When he arrived in Battle to become Abbot of St Martin (1175 - 1200) monks and burgesses alike flocked to conduct him into town and the burgesses crowded into the chapter house to hear their new Abbot's first sermon.

31. The magnificent grounds of Battle Abbey were thrown open in the last century and excursion trains were run to the town. This photograph shows some of the beauty of these grounds with a pupil from Battle Abbey school gazing in the water of the monks' stew pond, with other pupils standing by their horses; in the background may be seen the ruins and in particular the roofless dorter. *c.*1935.

32. (*above*) An aerial view of Battle Abbey. On the left of the picture is the Green with a cluster of houses surrounding it. Also shown is the precinct wall running from the Gatehouse towards the church. The buildings in the centre are those occupied by the girls' school, while the roofless dorter (the monks' dormitory) of the original monastery lies behind. On the right are the remains of Sir Anthony Browne's 16th century mansion, the twin towers and upper terrace.

ISAAC INGALL,

Who lived in LADY WEBSTER'S *Family at Battle Abbey,*
Sussex, where he had been a domestic upwards
of 90 Years.

Died April 2nd 1798, Aged 120 Years.

33. Isaac Ingall was an ancient retainer of the Webster family. He is reputed to have lived to 120. He also asserted that he had been serving the family for upwards of a century. He was active to the last, walking about supported on two stout sticks.

34. The Library was in the first instance built for the reception of Queen Elizabeth I but was remodelled by Mr. Clutton (the architect responsible for much of the Victorian work carried out at the Abbey). It was a very large room, but had been even longer in the past; the dimensions in 1877 were 76 feet by 23 feet. The parquet floor and the whole of the woodwork (book-cases, chimney-piece, roof) were all executed to the design of Mr. Clutton and carried out by Messrs. Ruddel of Peterborough. There appeared to be no catalogue of the library. This picture dates from *c.* 1890.

35. Battle Abbey: A view of the interior, showing the sumptuously furnished apartments during the life-time of the Duke and Duchess of Cleveland. Much of the furniture in the room had been collected by the Duchess. The sofas and the chair coverings were of flowered Genoese cotton and on one wall hung an Aubusson tapestry, much prized by the Clevelands.

36. The Abbot's Hall was described by the Duchess of Cleveland as 'a grandly proportioned hall. . . it measures 57 feet 9 inches in length, 31 feet in breadth, and 57 feet in height'. Grimm painted it in 1783.

37. (*left*) Harry George, 4th Duke of Cleveland, was born 19 April 1803, and married Catherine Lucy Wilhelmina, widow of Archibald, Lord Dalmeny, and only daughter of the 4th Earl Stanhope. As Lord Harry Vane, he bought the Abbey in 1859 from Sir Augustus Webster. He obtained a royal licence granting him and his issue leave to take the surname of Powlett only (instead of the patronymic Vane) and to bear the coat of arms of the family of Powlett. A contemporary report described the Duke as "a fine specimen of an English aristocrat and as he grew older his picturesqueness increased, one of the 28 noblemen who in 1883 possess above 100,000 acres in the U.K." He died in 1891.

38. The Duchess of Cleveland on the white donkey given to her by Lord Kitchener, riding along the High Street of Battle. *c.* 1895. The local children used to shout when they saw her "here comes the Duchess riding on her ass"! The building on the left (the Almonry) is one of the oldest houses in the town, although largly refaced above the ground floor.

39. David Potter, guide at Battle Abbey for a number of years, *c.* 1931. The
Duchess of Cleveland was responsible for opening Battle Abbey to the public in
the last century. Special excursion trains were run from Hastings; more than
800 visitors came on one Tuesday, between 11 a.m. until 5 p.m.

40. These gargoyles formerly adorned the wall of the Gateway but were later placed in the grounds of Battle Abbey.

41. The obverse side of the Abbey Seal of the deed of surrender represents the western end of a large and handsome church within a border, in which are the words *Sigillum Conventus Sancti Martini de Bello* (shown here). The reverse side has a picture of St Martin dividing his cloak with a naked beggar. It is thought that the church on this seal may have been that belonging to the Abbey.

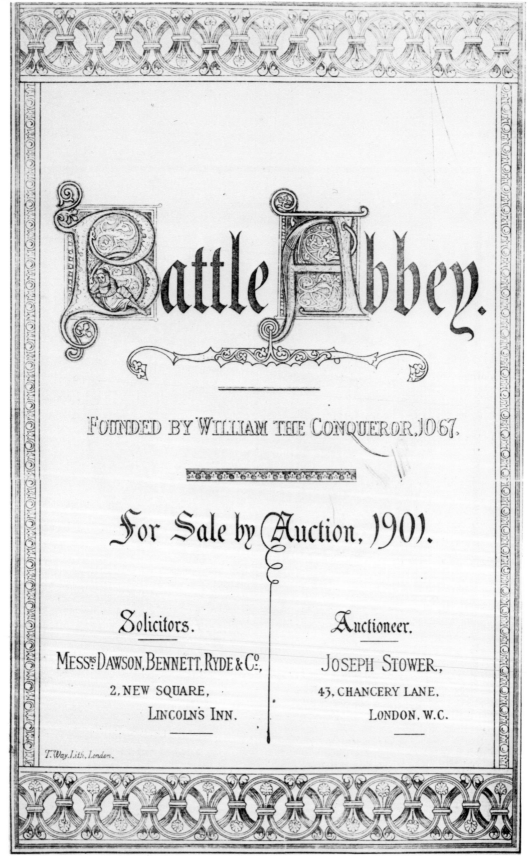

Battle Abbey.

FOUNDED BY WILLIAM THE CONQUEROR, 1067.

For Sale by Auction, 1901.

Solicitors.	Auctioneer.
MESSRS. DAWSON, BENNETT, RYDE & CO.,	JOSEPH STOWER.,
2, NEW SQUARE,	43, CHANCERY LANE,
LINCOLN'S INN.	LONDON, W.C.

T. Way, Lith, London.

42. and 43. Front Cover and (*opposite page*) General Summary of the Battle Abbey Sale

GENERAL SUMMARY.

BATTLE ESTATE—
(as shewn on Plan no. 1).

	Quantity. A.	R.	P.	Rental. £	s.	d.
The Abbey, Ruins, Gardens, Park, &c.	159	1	6	In hand		
House Property in the Town	44	1	16	554	7	9
Drill Hall	0	2	0	75	0	0
Cattle Market	0	0	30	10	0	0
The Wellington Inn and Lands.............................	21	0	21	160	0	0
Fern Lea House, King's Head Windmill, &c.	3	3	13	70	0	0
Caldbec Hill Cottages and Lands	4	0	20	48	6	0
Park Dale House, Grounds and Lands...................	65	0	18	134	0	0
Powder Mill Lake and Farthing Pond	11	1	5	In hand		
Two Cottages near	0	1	14	5	4	0
Farms, Small Holdings and Cottages	2199	1	17	2206	4	6
Woods and Plantations	1156	2	25	In hand		
Sporting over about 2000 Acres, with Keeper's Cottage...	0	3	3	54	0	0
Battle Great Tithes				133	1	7

EWHURST AND NORTHIAM PORTIONS—
(as shewn no Plan no. 2).

Farms and Holdings, including Joint Sporting Rights...	1193	3	21	815	0	0
Woods and Plantations	258	1	27	In hand		
Great Tithes—Ewhurst Parish				97	16	2
Hop ditto „				14	9	7

BEXHILL-ON-SEA AND HOOE PORTIONS—
(as shewn on Plan no. 3).

Farms and Small Holdings	897	3	30	970	7	0
Woods and Plantations	51	3	15	In hand		
Sporting Rights				40	0	0

PETT PORTION—
(as shewn on addition to Plan no. 1).

Marsh Lands..	48	1	23	115	0	0

Total Acreage of the Battle Abbey Estate   6117 1 24

Catalogue, dated 1901. Sir Augustus Webster repurchased it from the Duke of Cleveland for £200,000.

44. Church of St Mary the Virgin. This engraving, which could be by Rowe, *c*.1830, also shows the excavations of the Abbey church in progress.

Church of St Mary the Virgin

45. Contrasting wall surrounding the Church of St Mary, Battle. In the year 1270 Bishop Anian of St Aspal granted an indulgence of 20 days to all who contributed to the building of this church, and the following year it became known as the parish church. *c*.1900.

46. St Mary the Virgin's Church, Battle, founded between 1107 and 1124 by Ralph the 3rd abbot. It is partly Norman, but mainly early English with decorated and perpendicular additions. The font is Norman with a medieval cover. The tower was rebuilt where it now stands about 1450. The interior of the church was over-restored by Butterfield in the last century, but many of the treasures remain, including ancient glass depicting Archbishop Chicheley, an aumbry for the Communion vessels and two piscinae for cleansing the Communion vessels. In the chapel of St Catherine on the pillar behind the dean's stall are small crosses such as those made by the Crusaders on their return from fighting the Saracens; also the markings where they blunted the points of their swords. From these we estimate that there were three Crusaders from this district; two may have been the sons of Osbert FitzRalph of Bodiam, as it is recorded that they performed their vigil at Battle before setting out on their Crusade.

47. A sketch of the interior of St Mary's, showing the mural before Butterfield's restoration of 1869. After being obliterated by limewash at the Reformation in the early 16th century, the paintings were rediscovered and partly exposed some 300 years later. All are now destroyed except for a scrap or two in the chancel, and the remains of the north nave wall series. The drawings were of exceptional quality.

48. Drawing by W. H. Brooke showing a section of Battle Church. The pillars in the nave are transitional Norman (1170/1230). At the east end these have floral decorations on the capitals and are earlier than those at the other end. Over the arches are the outlines of wall paintings of the 13th century. In the south window may be seen the figure of Dean Clere in a red cope. The box pews were removed in the last century at the time of the Butterfield restoration.

49. Often refered to as the 'dorter', this large structure was erected in the 12th century. It is the largest remaining fragment of the original structure, and although now isolated, was once connected with the main building. It was thought that the building was used as a refectory and in some prints it is referred to as such whilst the dormitory for the monks was in the lower portion. However, other sources state that from the interior walls it can be seen that the dorter was broken into cells, and each monk had a cell with a window. In this picture the tall lancet windows can be appreciated; they are typical of the early English period. This photograph shows an art group from the school, studying in the ruins c.1935. After serving for centuries as a monastic apartment, this immense room, 150 feet long and 35 feet broad, was successively used as a barn and a stable. It was to enable the horses to pass in and out that the ground was raised to the level of its turf-grown floor. The old roof fell in during the early years of the 19th century, but a diminishing quantity of the ancient plaster still clings to the venerable walls. Nothing remains of the original tiled floor, part of which was visible as late as 1811. (see plate no.28)

50. and 51. Newly discovered ancient features revealed during restoration work on Battle Abbey School following the disastrous fire of 1931.

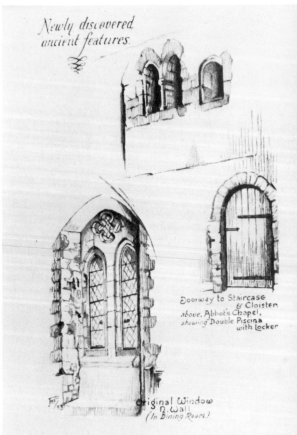

52. and 53. The smouldering timbers of Battle Abbey School in 1931; the first photograph shows the damaged roof with the Gateway in the background, and the other in the interior of the Great Hall. After this disaster the school spent two years in exile. The restoration work was conducted by Sir Harold Brakspear and many discoveries were made, including an exquisite double piscine, a secret wall staircase leading from the Beggars' Hall to the Abbot's Hall and a second chapel with a window communicating with the Abbot's bedroom. The school was re-opened by the Bishop of Chichester in the presence of the late Princess Alice, Countess of Athlone, and many other distinguished guests.

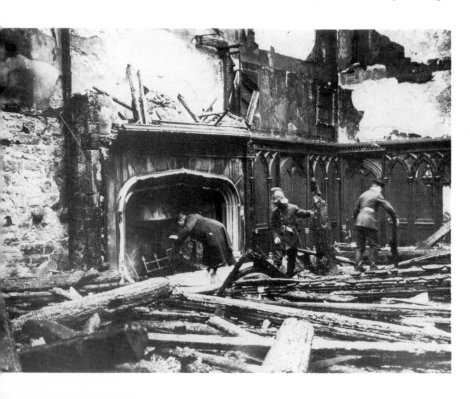

Ashburnham Place

54. (*above*) This aerial view shows the magnificent 90 room mansion of Ashburnham Place in the 1930s, during the lifetime of the last direct descendant Lady Catherine Ashburnham. (*copyright: Airviews Ltd.*)

55. (*opposite*) The Earls of Ashburnham lived in the area for nearly 800 years. At the time of the compilation of Domesday, Ashburnham was held by Robert de Cruel, or as the name is more commonly written De Criol. Before the Conquest the owner was one Seward. He is not otherwise recorded but Ashburnham was wasted by the Conqueror (its value was reduced from six pounds to twenty shillings.) In the cellars of Ashburnham Place (partially demolished in 1960) are parts of stonework thought to date from the 15th century. By 1638 the house may have been a moated manor. The first recorded view of Ashburnham, by Leonard Knyff, shows a mid-Georgian house added to a square Charles II building, about 1700. In 1815-16 the building was refaced in the "Gothic" manner with pinnacles and turrets, but later in the 19th century the facade began to crumble and Bertram, 4th Earl of Ashburnham, decided to reface the building in handmade bricks from the estate brickyard. At this time the height of the state apartments were raised thus throwing out the classical lines of the earlier house. The magnificent grounds were laid out by Capability Brown, the well-known landscape gardener. (*copyright: Country Life Publications Ltd.*)

56. The magnificent stone staircase at Ashburnham Place, now, sadly, demolished, which led up to a galleried first floor. From this, two subsidiary staircases led up again to a higher floor, also galleried. The ironwork was the work of William Bourd under the architect George Dance's direction. The siting of two cast-iron stoves on the grand staircase was one of the principal reasons for the quarrel and final break between the architect and the 3rd Earl. George Dance had been employed by the Earl to carry out extensive improvements at Ashburnham Place between 1812 and 1817. (*copyright: Country Life Publications Ltd.*)

57. (*below*) Displayed in Ashburnham Church for a number of years was the linen vest worn by King Charles I on the scaffold, and the watch given by him to his friend 'Jack Ashburnham. Sadly these articles were removed for safe keeping as the case of the watch was stolen in the last century. (*copyright: Country Life Publications Ltd.*)

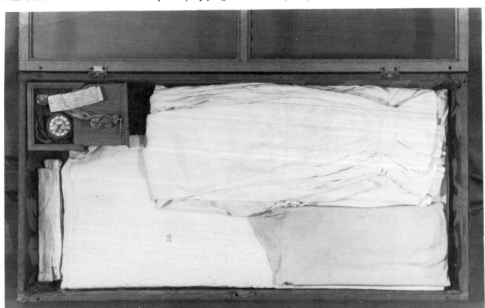

58. and 59. (*left and below*) Two contrasting studies of Bertram, 4th Earl of Ashburnham. The painting of him as a young man is by an unknown artist. The later picture, *c.* 1876, shows him in front of his Sussex seat, Ashburnham Place, attended by one of his six surviving sons and a groom. Some of the day's 'bag' is on the ground while more is carried by the two attendants.

60. A family photograph, reputed to have been taken by Katherine Ashburnham (daughter of the 4th Earl), which shows her six surviving brothers in front of their ancestral home, Ashburnham Place. Bertram, the eldest and later the 5th Earl, is on the left and George the youngest at the right-hand side. Unfortunately it has been impossible to identify with any degree of accuracy the four middle figures, one of whom, Thomas, after Bertram's death in 1913 inherited the estate, becoming the 6th and last Earl of Ashburnham. In this photograph can be seen part of Ashburnham Place showing the elaborate brickwork in which it was refaced in 1853-55. In the background can be seen the old clock tower. *c.*1875.

Normanhurst Court

61. (*above*) "Normanhurst" (sometimes called "Normanhurst Court") was built in the style of a French chateau for Thomas, Lord Brassey, a railway magnate. When built, it was one of the most recent of the "stately homes of England"; the foundation was laid in 1865, and the work completed in 1871. The French-style roofs were constructed with cast-iron palisades around the top. The clock tower was fitted with musical bells, and the stables were complete with a covered drive in order that the horses could be exercised during inclement weather. Thomas Brassey himself died before the house was completed. Thomas Brassey II, his eldest son, lived there with his wife. He was 20 years Liberal M.P. for Hastings.

62. The Pompeian Room at Normanhurst Court.

POMPEAN ROOM.
NORMANHURST COURT
17359

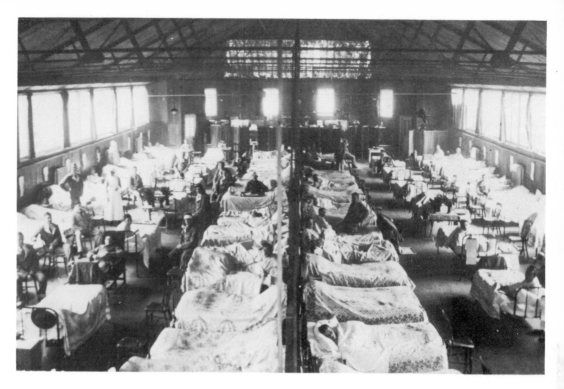

63. Indoor tennis court at Normanhurst. During World War I this large building was converted into a hospital ward. As will be seen from the photograph, all available space was utilised.

64. Lady Idina Brassey, the Commandant and some of the nurses at Normanhurst, nr. Battle. c.1916.

65. The Brassey family on their yacht Sunbeam. From L. to R. : young Thomas Brassey; his sisters Mabelle and Marie Adelaide; Lady Brassey and another daughter Muriel. The two younger girls became Countess De La Warr, and Lady Willingdon. The picture was taken *c.*1886-7.

66. and 67. Two items relating to the Brassey Family of Normanhurst Court. (*left*) A menu card and (*below*) an invitation card.

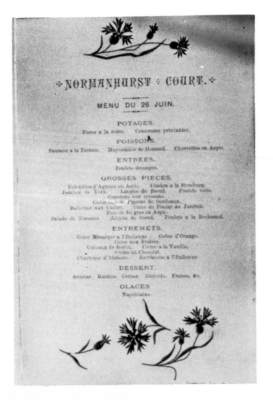

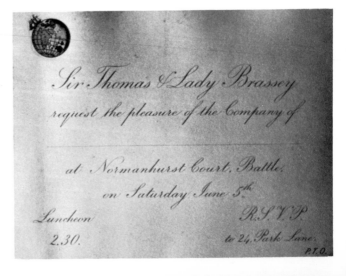

8. On Sunday 2 August 1908 a fire broke out in one of the maids'
bedrooms at Normanhurst, despite the fact that the house was thought
to be of fireproof construction and had water-supplying hydrants at
frequent intervals. Fire engines raced from nearby towns including
Bexhill and Hastings, in order to reinforce the local one from Battle;
it was said they took so long to arrive that Lord Brassey decided the
house should have its own fire engine in future!

69. A parade of Scouts *c.*1938 passing the premises of Tills the ironmongers of Battle. In this photograph the old shop front of the building can be seen. The firm has been in operation since the 16th century, and has carried on its business from the same premises.

70. A view of William C. Till, Ltd. ironmongers of Battle showing the facade. William Hammond, was the first recorded proprietor in the 18th century. However in the year 1538 one John Hammond, the last Abbot of Battle Abbey, was said to have started in business in a street near by. This is conjecture, as the clergy in those days were not permitted to engage in trade, but he may well have been connected with the Hammonds who became proprietors of the business when the actual records commence.

71. Another view of William C. Till, Ltd. This one shows the original doorway.

72. (*left*) This picture shows the interior of the ironmongers before modernisation.

73. A page from the ledger of William C. Till, Ltd., which was in use between the years 1716 and 1732. There are no actual records before then. The entries show business done at Rye and Pevensy (*sic*) and one entry is of great interest, for on June 28th 1719, it runs "Abrose Juke of Dudle in Wostershear for a paier smis belos £2.10.0d." Apparently bad debts were made in those days, for only £1.1s.0d. was received on account, the balance being left unpaid.

74. A photograph of the shop of C. Turner early in this century. It offered a variety of goods from 'New Milk' to Fry's Chocolate and jars of sweets. The sign above the doorway states that Mr. C. Turner also carried on the trade of 'Printer and Bookbinder' at no. 53 High Street.

75. Alex Vicary, his brother, and another man outside their Cycle Shop, *c.*1920. Later they sold cars and petrol. The original founders of this firm were Mr. Chatfield and Mr. Cook.

76. A South-East and Chatham Railway waggon turning from Mount Street into High Street. The driver was Mr. Charles Holland, who was employed in this capacity for a number of years. *c.*1915.

77.   During the First World War Mr. Jack Bailey launched the Battle Rabbitjack Cottage Industry to meet
the demand for the old rabbit-skin caps caused by war shortage. About 90 persons were employed and orders
were even placed by London stores, Originally, Mr. Paul Pemble had had a business in the High Street making
these same hats, leather gloves and gaiters. He also made penny cricket balls, one of which is in the Battle
Museum. Mr. Dunn, the postmaster, was reputed to be the last man in Battle to wear a 'Battlejack'. This
photograph shows Mr. Bailey at work (1919).

78. The Old Blacksmith's Forge in Mount Street.

79. Interior of the Forge. On the right may be seen the blacksmith, Mr. Tom Beney, who went to work at the forge in 1891, when it was run by a Mr. Payne from whom he took over in 1895. He remained there until he retired in 1949. In his heyday, Mr. Beney employed four men and kept three fires going. Later the forge became an engineering works.

80.   The original *King's Head Inn* was on Caldbec Hill in the house now known as Wellington House, originally called Friars Halt, where part of the foundations can still be seen.

81. The Spillway at Ashburnham Forge, *c.*1900. Ashburnham Iron Works were the last of the great Sussex works to close in 1813. However, the forge continued to operate a few years longer; finally ceasing in 1830. It was particularly renowned for its ironbacks, railings and graveslabs. Earlier in its history it had produced cannons, one of which may be seen today in Pevensey Castle with the mark of the Ashburnham Ironworks on its barrel, this being a Tudor Rose. Behind the dam there was originally a pond which was said to be over 12 acres in size, but it was drained sometime in the 1820s and is now used for grazing.

82. The Powdermills and Grounds at Battle. In 1814 a beam engine was installed at the "House" to supplement the water power; note the chimney. A pre 1816 lithograph.

83. The scene at Powdermill Pond in 1956, showing the cottage which housed the millwright when the gunpowder industry was situated here.

Gunpowder

For 200 years the manufacture of gunpowder flourished at Battle. In 1676, John Hammond was granted 'four parcels of brookland and upland, called Peperengeye Lands in Battle with permission to erect a Powder Mill.' At one time there were five mills on the River Asten, each using the same water in succession, the best known of which were 'Farthing', 'House' (as the Powdermill site was known) and half a mile downstream 'Peppering-Eye' (*sic*). The reputation of Battle powder was very high. Defoe mentioned that the town was remarkable for making "the finest gunpowder, and the best, perhaps, in Europe." The process of manufacture remained fairly constant over the years. Throughout England only 40 pounds of powder was allowed to be made at one time under one pair of stones but Battle was the exception to this rule; and it may have been a contributory factor to the many explosions that occurred locally. One, for instance, was in 1798, when a vast explosion killed three men and destroyed seven houses. The last fatal explosion was in 1808 when 200 barrels of gunpowder, and several buildings were destroyed. Two men and a child were killed. The closing of the mills in the middle of the last century seems to have been due to the refusal of the Duke of Cleveland to renew the lease because of the frequent explosions.

84. Mr. James Morgan aged 96 years outside the Watch Houses at Powdermill. Mr. Morgan had the dangerous job of taking the powder in a horse drawn waggon to Dartford and other places, usually more than a day's journey from Battle. He was the last surviving employee of the Mills. On the left of the photograph may be seen the old saltpetre refiring cistern. The small building behind the cistern was the 'charge' room. *c.*1918.

85. View of runner stones, on site of Pepper-in -Eye Mills, with old glazing house powder building beyond. Glazing was the fifth process in the making of powder; the powder grains were rotated in barrels with a little plumbago, and this produced the characteristic polish of gunpowder.

86. A scene still visible today in the woods surrounding Battle, but the bark is no longer used by the tanning industry. c.1900.

87.   Demolition of the old tanyard in Battle, 1955.

88.   17th century house, later faced with brick on the ground floor and tile hung above. The shoe shop was started in 1813. As early as the 12th century 'The Chronicle of Battle Abbey' records that four shoemakers were working in Battle. It is thought that the monks were responsible for starting the tannery and it is likely that they taught the people the art of leatherworking. Even as late as the 19th century bark from trees was still used in the local industry, and skins were collected from all parts of the county. This picture shows Thorpe & Co. Note the boots hanging outside the shop, a favourite form of advertising one's goods in the past. The boy standing in the doorway may be Tom Pook who worked in the shop all his life under Harry Sinden, who married the boss's daughter and later in his career became 'governor'. c.1900.

89. J. Holland, butcher. At this time (*c.*1890) the premises were in Upper Lake, Battle. It is interesting to note that hygiene did not play much part in everyday life, as a garland of sausages may be seen forming part of the decoration! The shop was obviously a busy one, as three of the men were wearing the traditional butchers' apron.

90. Mr. Slatter, butcher of 10 High Street, father of the founder of Allworks' grocery business carried on at 72 High Street. *c.*1780.

91. Mr. and Mrs. Jenner proceeding along the High Street and passing a horse-drawn waggon unloading at R.B. Allwork & Son.

92. Comparison may be made between this picture showing the new shop front and the earlier one shown in the picture above. The two Mr. Allworks are shown here outside the premises.

93. The staff of Allworks outside the shop, *c.* 1924. Next to Allworks were the offices of Newbery's the jam makers, and the building next to this was Dr. Kendall's private house and surgery.

94. Battle Post Office, when it was situated in the High Street, showing the facade decorated in honour of Queen Victoria's Diamond Jubilee 1897. Mr J.T. Dunn (tailor, habit maker and woollen draper) and his brother are standing outside the main doorway. He was the Postmaster from 1871 until the end of the century. In the window can be seen the old clock, designed like a watch, which today is in Battle Museum.

95. Battle Post Office, 1900. On the left is Mr. Muggridge, and on the right Mr. Glenisher, two local postmen.

96. A scene typical of farming in the last century. This picture shows a yoke of oxen at Pepper-in-Eye Farm, Battle. Shortly after this picture was taken they were sent for slaughter, and the farmer changed to horses for ploughing and general farm work, being one of the last to do so.

97. Levelling the ground for Battle Cricket Club pitch, at the rear of the High Street on the south-west side.

98. The town obtained milk from nearby farms. This picture, *c.*1920, shows churns being loaded. The man on the left was George Keywood and the lady in the cart Mrs. Wood.

99. Mr. Hannay with a milk float at St. Mary's Farm. The horse was bought from Ben Gosden, the butcher, and was understood to be very quiet. One day it was pulled up outside Chapel Cottages, when a train went under the railway bridge, the horse bolted, knocking over a lamp-post; whilst the horse survived the impact, the cart was damaged beyond repair. However, it was not used again in the shafts for delivery of milk. Mr. Hannay had previously bred goats and delivered their milk in goat carts! *c.*1920.

100.   This photograph shows Mrs. Harris who delivered milk for Widdecombe Dairy. *c.*1935.

101.   The large ivy-clad building on the right is Langton House, built in 1569. Between 1718-1724 it was the poorhouse, but about 1730 it passed into the hands of the Hammond family. Their daughter married David Langton - hence its present name - and after the death of the last Langton in 1805, the house seems once more to have become the town's poorhouse. In 1829 it passsed into the hands of the schoolmaster William Ticehurst; his descendants occupied it until 1922. In 1902, however, the house was divided, the portion where the Ticehurst family lived acquiring their name whilst the remainder retained the old name of Langton House. In 1960 the whole building became the Battle Memorial Hall, and it now also houses the Battle Museum.

102.   This photograph shows both sides of the High Street *c.* 1920.

103. Top of High Street, c.1900. The building in the far distance on the left-hand side of the picture has an 18th century front to a much older structure. It is on the site of the guildhall of the Mountjoy Guild, one of the town's three medieval buildings, and below it are the original 14th century vaulted cellars. In the interior there is an excellent example of a dragon beam.

104. This photograph shows private houses built in the worst possible taste between 1898 and 1902 adjoining Langton House - these replaced interesting old shops of a previous age.

105. This picture shows the High Street decorated for Edward VII's Coronation celebrations.

106. A corner of the Abbey Green and Langton House decorated for the Coronation of
Edward VII. 1902.

107. One of the few photographs in existence showing a brewer's dray outside the Battle brewery. In 1828 the brewer was Charles A. Goodwin and from 1887-1911 Mr. Bailey.

108. The entrance to the brewery, with Mr. Holland a drayman standing in the archway. Although the chimney has been demolished it is still possible to view the old brewery buildings through this arch which was next to the old London & County Joint Stock Bank.

109. Described in the 12th century *Chronicle of Battel Abbey* as 'The House of Pilgrims, which is called the Hospital.' It was rebuilt about 1420, and well restored in the 1930s. It is a fine example of a typical Wealden framed hall house. Note that the right-hand end is of later date, probably early 16th century.

110. The main entrance to the hospital, formerly the workhouse. In 1902 it was reported that 60 gallons of high quality spirit was consumed daily at the workhouse; the doctor in charge replied that he only gave it to these inmates when they were run down and "they found these people drooping for want of it but when allowed they perked up and got better."

111.   A view of the Wellington Hotel.

112.   This picture shows Mount Street looking towards Caldbec Hill. The *King's Head Inn* has a comparatively modern front to an older, possibly timber, building. In the 18th century this inn was at the top of Caldbec Hill, near the mill. It might have moved down when Mount Street ceased to be the main London Road.

113. Mount Street, looking towards the High Street. The photograph shows the street decorated for the coronation of Edward VII, in August 1902. Mount Street displays a medley of styles; one of its more renowned houses is the Crooked House.

114. Upper Lake early this century. The cottages on the left originally extended eastwards from the precinct wall of Battle Abbey and are the remains of a 19 bay range. It is thought that they were erected by the Abbey as a speculative venture during the second half of the 15th century. (See: *Historic Buildings in Eastern Sussex No.1* pp. 3-4)

115. Upper Lake, showing the row of 'Wealden' houses on the right hand side of the photograph, also the premises of Holland, the butcher. c.1900.

116. Lower Lake, c.1920. The row of houses on the left of the photograph are estate dwellings, originally built by Battle Abbey Estate.

BATTLE.

TO BE SOLD BY AUCTION,

BY

MR. C. H. SMITH,

AT THE

CHEQUERS INN, BATTLE,

On Tuesday, August 10, 1852,

At Four o'clock in the Afternoon, in One Lot;

A DWELLING HOUSE,

In the Lower Lake, Battle, in Three Tenements;

In the several occupations of George Reed, Benjamin Hesman, and James Tompsett. With a Garden extending behind, and containing by admeasurement one rood and eleven perches.

ALSO, A

WHEELWRIGHT'S SHED,

In the occupation of the said George Reed.

The above Premises are copyhold of the Manor of Battle, and subject to an annual Quit Rent of three shillings, and a Fine at Will on death or alienation.

The Property is advantageously situate in the Main Road of the Town of Battle, within a few minutes walk of the Railway Station, and offers an eligible opportunity either for investment or building.

For further Particulars and to view apply to Mr. William Metcalf; on the premises; Mr. W. Noakes, Battle; Mr. N. P. Kell, Solicitor, Battle; or to the Auctioneer, Hurstgreen, Sussex.

F. W. TICEHURST, PRINTER, BATTLE.

117. A sale bill for a Battle house.

118. Lake House, 1890, home of the Noakes family who
owned Battle Tanyard. Whilst this building is still in existence
today it is much altered. This is the junction of Upper and
Lower Lake.

119. A view of part of the Abbey by James Rouse: early 19th century.

THE ILLUSTRATED LONDON NEWS.

TUNBRIDGE WELLS AND HASTINGS RAILWA

120. *(above)* Railway Bridge, *c.*1920. On the right hand side may be glimpsed the Wesleyan Chapel, Lower Lake, built in the last century. Beyond this on the hill stands the old tannery.

121. *(centre)* Battle Station was built by the famous railway architect William Tress, and opened in January 1852. It was designed to harmonise with the town, and it is an excellent example of Victorian Gothic.

122. *(below)* The railway station today.

123. A steam locomotive waiting to depart.

124. The Deanery, which is located behind the church. It is of brick and was originally a two storey building. It is considered to date from before the 17th century, although its rainwater butts are dated 1669.

125. The Grammar School, later 'The Tower Hotel' (now demolished). The 1871 census showed William Lamborn as head of the Grammar School. From the census this appears to have had 30 boys, ranging in age from 9-16 years.

126. The Police Station built in 1861 is a remarkably fine structure. Previously they occupied the 'House of Correction' in Lower Lake. At one time this station contained one of the few remaining two-tiered cell blocks but this was removed when the interior was modernised.

127. The Superintendent of Police in his pony trap, outside the old Courthouse. c.1914. P. C. Webb, who acted as groom, always complained that Superintendent Plumm, who was a big man, weighing nearly 20 stone, would insist on sitting too far back in the trap thereby raising the shafts!

128. and 129.   Bexhill-on-Sea   was connected to Battle via the opening of the Crowhurst — Bexhill
West line in 1902. One of the greatest engineering feats was the building of a viaduct over the Crowhurst
marshes. The line was closed in 1964, and the viaduct demolished in 1969.

130. Rocks Gate, Battle.

131. At one time this was the main Hastings/London Road via Battle, and wayfarers no doubt refreshed themselves at this old inn called the *Black Horse. c.*1920.

132. (*below*) A peaceful scene early this century on one of the lanes leading from Crowhurst to Battle. Crowhurst powdermill was on the same stream as the Battle ones, and included in the complex.

133. At one time windmills dotted the skyline of Battle, there being six within a radius of one mile; sadly today only one remains - Battle Mill or King's Head Mill on Caldbec Hill, which was converted into a private house in 1924.

134. Three paintings executed by Francis Grose in 1787, during his tour
through the Sussex countryside.

135. Newbery's delivery van. The boy on the right hand side of the vehicle is Dave Gander and the driver
is thought to be L. Hutchinson. It will be noticed that due to the icy conditions underfoot a chock has
been placed on the back wheels of the vehicle. c.1920.

136. Mr. William H. Wheaton with his young son Victor in his highly decorated van carrying on his trade as ironmonger and colourman.

137. Mr. Percy Boxall in his first job as 'the donkey milkman.' At the time this photograph was taken skimmed milk sold for ½d. a pint. Later in his life this young man was employed as chauffeur to Lady Catherine Ashburnham of Ashburnham Place.

Battle Abbey Pageant

Pageant Master - Gwen Lally

4th to 16th
July, 1932
(inclusive, excepting Sunday)

Every Evening
At 7 p.m.

Matinees :

Wednesdays

and

Saturdays

At 3 p.m.

The action is set on the site of the
Battle of Hastings 1066, in the Grounds of
BATTLE ABBEY, SUSSEX

(By kind permission of Miss Webster and Mrs. Jacoby)

Master of the Music

Organising Director

JAMES R. DEAR, Mus. Bac.

Mrs. A. SHAW-MACKENZIE

139. —143. Various photographs of the pageant organised by Gwen Lally in 1932. Unfortunately, this event was not a financial success because of the high cost of hiring the elaborate costumes. Many people from surrounding villages took part, together with the inhabitants of Battle and girls from Battle Abbey School.

138. (*opposite page*) Poster advertising the Battle Abbey Pageant of July 1932.

Battle Abbey Pageant

144.   A colourful pageant was organised by Bexhill Round Table in 1966 to commemorate 1066; a re-enactment of the Battle of Hastings, fought on the original site, between students from Sussex University (who were the Norman foes) and those from the University of Kent (as Saxons), backed up by young riders on their ponies. On the left is Heather Freeman and on the right Avia Guilmant. (Reproduced by kind permission of George Gregory).

145. and 146. Two early photographs of a 'Meet' on the Abbey Green. The 'modern' East Sussex Hunt dates from 1853, but there had been a pack of hounds of this name hunting as early as 1826.

147. Unfortunately it has been impossible to identify these two young riders attended by their grooms but this Meet is at one of the large houses in the Battle area. It may be that the young man on the donkey may be the same one as in picture no. 146. *c.* 1900.

COPY OF ENTRY IN REGISTER OF MOTOR CARS.

The following is a correct Copy of the Entry in the Register of Motor Cars relating to Motor Car No. DY 86

Index Mark and Number on Identification Plate. (1)	Full Name of Owner, and Postal Address of his usual Residence. (2)	Description or Type of Car. (3)	Type and Colour of Body of Car. (4)	Weight Unladen. (5)	Whether intended for			Date of Registration. (7)	If Cancelled, Date of Cancellation. (8)
					Private Use.	Use for Trade Purposes.	Use as a Public Conveyance.		
DY. 86.	William Alfred Jenner 56 High Street Battle	6 h.p. 4 seated (Own make)	Vis a Vis body painted dark green	8 cwt	—	—	2/10	1904 25th April	

Dated 25th April 1904   Signed Ben. F. ......

148. (*top*) Mr. Jenner, seen here with his wife, decided to build a car in 1892, but it was not completed until 1901. It was made in Battle with the exception of the rough castings for crank case, cylinder and tyres. On a run of 100 miles no punctures or breakdown occurred, a truly magnificent achievement for the time.

149. The Motor Car Registration Act came into force in 1903 and Mr. Jenner's 'Vis a Vis' 6 h.p. 'Senlac' was registered in 1904 under the registration no. DY 86.

150. A different view of Battle Abbey Green, on the occasion of a Boxing Day Meet c.1930. Note that many of the cars appear to be the same model.

151. (centre) The cycling boom reached its peak in the 1890s and many clubs sprang into being. It is interesting to note that no lady cyclist is present. c.1900.

152. A 'Meet' outside the Station Hotel c.1904. Mrs. Hale (with her back to the camera) ran out from the inn still holding the bread and cheese she was eating at the time! The back coach was Skinners' 'Royal Sovereign' from Hastings, and in front of it was the 'John Bull', owned by Martens of Bohemia.

153. and 154.   Two well known buses which operated in the Battle area during and after the First World War. One was called the 'Battle Queen' and the other 'Pride of Battle'. The first bus, which covered the route from Sidley to Battle via the villages of Ninfield and Catsfield, was converted from a Ford Trixi. This picture shows the bus standing outside the old steam laundry. The other picture shows the Battle Choir on their annual 'outing'. The bus was driven and owned by Mr. Collin who at one time had a garage at Telham Hill. c.1922.

155. The headlines of the newspapers at the time of the 6th Earl of Ashburnham's death in 1924 entitled this picture "Peer's tragic homecoming". His coffin was borne on a farm wagon to the church followed by staff and tenants.

156. Battle Fire Brigade outside the Abbot's Hall, c.1920.

157. Mr. Raper, a well-known Battle solicitor, of the last century and the early part of this, leaving his office to return home. These premises are still occupied by the family firm of solicitors. *c.*1904.

158. Mr. Augustus Raper (usually known as "Gussie") outside his family home Pike House in Upper Lake (part of a complex of Wealden type houses). Mr. Raper is shown here standing beside his wife and flanked by his daughters.

159. Battle residents enjoying the sunshine. *c.*1900.

160. This photograph shows the victorious local football team. *c.*1910.

161. A Good Friday marbles match on the Abbey Green in the 1960s. This is a traditional game played through-out Sussex at this particular time of year. Members of one team dress in smock frocks. Other teams are less trad-ionally dressed, wearing football jerseys or even cloaks and bow ties.

162. Prospecting for the Battle water supply at Pepperingeye in 1900. A well was sunk and it was stated in a report that 'water was found at 270 feet before a government loan was granted' and 'it was proved by pumping 700 gallons an hour (day and night) for a fortnight.'

163. Outside the *George Hotel*, Battle. On the left is the head waiter, ostler and grooms.

164. Battle Langton Church of England School, founded in 1845. This photograph shows a class in the early part of the century. The boys from the workhouse were always easy to recognize by virtue of their heads being practically shaven.

165. (*opposite page, below*) Battle policemen on hop picking duty with the 'specials' (extra men recruited for this position during particularly busy periods). *c.*1910.

166. (*right*) 'The Bitter Bit'; Mr. H. Metson of Battle caught four rats in a trap in Pound Field near his chicken house. The next day he found the rats had disappeared and a stoat was in the trap. The picture shows him holding the stoat which was eventually drowned. *c.*1913.

167. (*below*) A peculiar address. This envelope was received by a Mrs. Boxall who lived in Black Horse Road, in 1913. It contained a letter from a gentleman in London stating that he and others with the Territorial Cyclists had called there where they had had some excellent lemonade, which he enjoyed so much that he wrote asking for directions to make it!

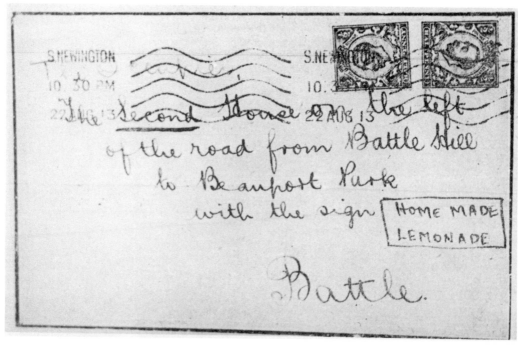

168. Longevity at Battle Workhouse. This photograph shows the old people at the workhouse over 80 years of age in 1913. They are, from left to right: (front row) Ann Russell 87; Julia McCartney 86; Sarah Chapman 84; (back row) Nurse Whitworth and Janette Walters 83; (men seated) Edwin Forster 82; Stephen Smith 82; John Wood 83; (men standing) James Harvey 81; George Clifton 82.

169. Caroline Mathews, Hawker of Battle, in the early years of this century. When her horse died she took her wares around in an old pram, still managing to travel miles around the district. c.1910.

170. An interesting experiment took place in Battle before World War I, when Mr. R. Rae ran a small mixed farm entirely on Canadian lines. Would-be emigrants were able to become pupils at this farm before taking up their grants of 160 acres of land in the New World. The photograph shows Mrs. Rae and her son on the steps of the bungalow.

171. Mrs. Rae at her American stove. *c.*1913.

174. (*above*) The old custom of burning Guy Fawkes is still kept up by "Ye Olde Battel (*sic*) Bonfire Society." The Battle Bonfire Boys head the torchlight parade, accompanied by brass bands; they display the huge effigy of Guy Fawkes, which appears year after year, whose head is believed to be over 150 years old. (1897).

175. (*right*) One of the most popular attractions of the Battle Bonfire Procession are the fancy costumes worn by many of the participants. At the 1913 Bonfire Mr. W. Butler wore this costume for over two hours, quite a remarkable feat considering its height was 16ft. 4ins.

172. and 173. (*opposite page*) Battle Fair was held on November 22. Cattle were sold privately by Welsh and Irish dealers, and on the Green a pleasure fair was held when all the local children were given a holiday from school. Matthias Slye of 'Sandbanks', Hailsham wrote in his diary for November 22 1808 "Battel Fair — Very full of Beast and Dull". He recorded his expenses for the day as 9s.6d.

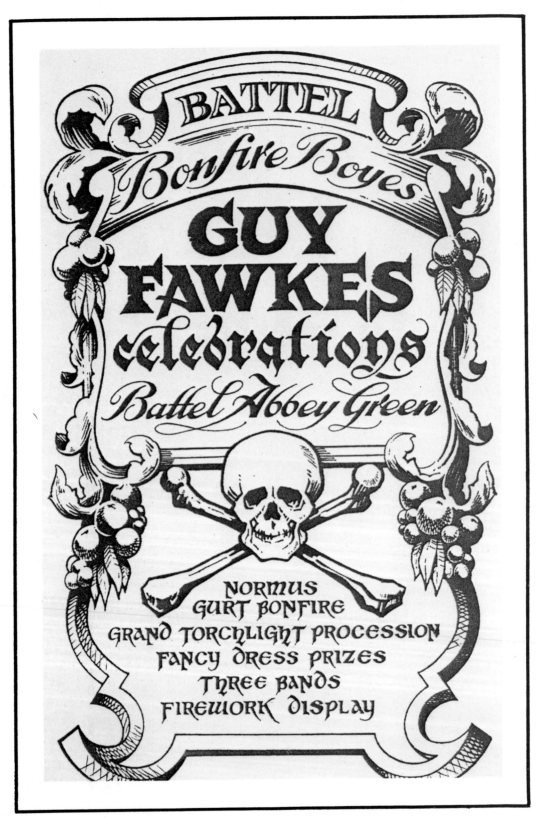

176.   Front cover of the 1982 programme.

177. The Queen and Prince Philip being greeted by Mrs. Harbord (nee Webster) on the 900th Anniversary of the Battle of Hastings. (*Evening Argus* and Battle Abbey School.)

TOWN of BATTLE

SUSSEX.

1860

J. W. Cole Surveyor.

178. Map showing the town plan of Battle in 1860.

CHRONOLOGICAL TABLE OF EVENTS IN THE HISTORY OF BATTLE ABBEY AND THE ABBEY ESTATE. 1066 TO THE PRESENT DAY

1066	Duke William of Normandy fought King Harold and obtained the crown of England.
1076	First Abbot of Battle, Gausbert, blessed by the Bishop of Chichester.
1094	Dedication of the Abbey by Archbishop Anselm in the presence of King William II (Rufus) and nobility.
1154–1188	Abbey Charters confirmed by Henry II following dispute between Abbot Walter and Bishop of Chichester.
1295	Abbot of Battle promoted to mitred rank with right to sit as a peer in the Lords.
1338	Abbot Alan de Ketling was allowed to fortify the Abbey because of French raids during this period. (The Hundred Years War began 1337.) Abbot Alan built the gateway.
1445	Chantry founded by Thomas, Lord of Hooe, at the altar of St Benignus in the Abbey church, for two priests to celebrate there for ever.
1538	Dissolution of the abbey.
1539	The king granted to Sir Anthony Browne the house and site of the late monastery of Battle.
1539–1719	The Viscounts Montague 'lost' 300 acres of Battle Great Park during the Civil War. The 5th Viscount pulled down the Abbey kitchens and sold the materials. The 6th Viscount sold the Abbey itself.
1719	Ownership of the Abbey Estate bought by Sir Thomas Webster, Bart.
1751	His son, Sir Whistler Webster, inherited; he reorganised the estate, but may have neglected and pulled down a part of the Abbey.
1810	Godfrey Vassal Webster inherited as a boy of ten. The estate was burdened and the Abbey in a ruinous condition. The dorter was converted into stables for a time, but new ones built in 1819.
1811–1817	Between these dates the Abbey Estates leased, likewise the Abbey itself in 1821.
1825	Sir Godfrey Webster was 'ruined'. £90,000 worth of timber sold, also the Abbey deeds and documents.
1858	Sir Augustus Webster sold the property to the future Duke of Cleveland, who died in 1891.
1901	Following the death of the Duchess of Cleveland, the 8th baronet, another Sir Augustus Webster bought back the Abbey. The Estate passed to Lucy Webster following the death in action during World War I of her only brother.
1922	Battle Abbey School took over buildings and grounds.
1931	Disastrous fire gutted Abbot's house.
1976	Battle Abbey taken over by Department of the Environment.

CHRONOLOGICAL TABLE OF EVENTS IN BATTLE TOWN

12th to 14th cent.	St Mary's church and tower erected.
1200	King John visited Battle.
1210	First mill recorded.
1246	First jail recorded.
1251	Schoolmaster at Battle mentioned in Battle Abbey Charters, 1 April 1251. This was a secular position, but may have been appointed by the Dean of Battle. By the reign of Elizabeth I Battle possessed a school and a schoolmaster. The elementary school was founded before 1800.
1264	Henry III came to Battle.
13th cent.	(mid). Battle became a centre for leather processing and working.
1295	Abbots of Battle summoned to parliament as peers.
1302	King Edward I visited Battle.
1324	King Edward III visited Battle.
14th cent.	Town crowded, still expanding until the second decade of the century. By the early 1330s the situation changed, and by 1340 there is slight evidence that the long trend was being reversed.
1331	High death rate suggests an epidemic.
1348/1350	(between). Black Death, population halved, estimated to be one thousand. The number of monks at the Abbey fell from 52 in 1347 to 34 in 1351-2.
1420	Pilgrims' Rest rebuilt. Described in the 12th century *Chronicle* of Battle Abbey as the 'House of Pilgrims'.
1450	During the Cade Rebellion a large contingent from Sussex joined Cade's Kentish followers. They included the Abbot of Battle with monks and servants; also certain gentlemen, one of whom was Lunsford of Battle.
1538	Dissolution of the Abbey. Sir Anthony Browne, Master of the King's Horse, enjoyed Henry VIII's favour, and took over Battle Abbey as his private residence in 1539.
1569	The Archbishop of Canterbury found Battle to be 'the most Popish town in all Sussex'.
15th to 17th cent.	The following were built: the *Bull* inn (now the *Nonsuch* hotel); the Deanery (after the Dissolution); the Almonry; Pike House, and the row of Wealden houses; Abbot Hamond's house; Langton House; and the Mountjoy Guild (14th century cellars).
1610	Church records commenced between 1610 and 1620.
1676	John Hamond of Battle obtained a 21-year lease of 'Peperynge Lands' (*sic*) with permission to erect a powder mill. Previous to this date an unauthorised powder mill had operated. One 'suppressed' in 1627 was operated by water.
c. 1660	Clockmaking commenced in Battle.
1721	His Majesty's forces stationed at Battle. Withdrawn 1722.
1729	Tornado struck the coast at Bexhill. Passed over Battle Great Wood. Subject of a London pamphlet.
1789	First nonconformist chapel built, demolished 1958.
1790–1805	Troops again stationed at Battle. Barracks built for the soldiers on the east side of Whatlington Road; demolished 1816.

1792 First mention of a lending library at Battle.
1798 Prince William of Gloucester ('Silly Billy') visited Isaac Ingall, to choose site for erection of the cavalry barracks.
1812 Closure of last Sussex ironworks at Ashburnham, near Battle.
1816 Duke of Wellington entertained by Sir Godfrey Webster at Battle Abbey.
1825 Battel [*sic*] Mechanics' Institute founded.
1830 William Cobbett, the Radical, on one of his 'Rural Rides' addressed the townsfolk of Battle. The town subsequently became one of the riot-centres of the campaign.
1834 Battle Union Workhouse built. Princess Victoria passed through town. First Battle Flower Show held in the Assembly Room at the *George* hotel (formerly an inn).
1836 Three local Turnpike Acts passed; the roads constructed included the Watch Oak/John's Cross road.
1838 Formation of The Battel [*sic*] Gas Co. for the purpose of lighting the town with gas. Re-registered as Battle Gas Co. 1871.
1845 The National and Langton Schools constructed in Marl-lane [*sic*] at a cost of £800; comprising two rooms about 36 feet by 18 feet wide, with a master's house between them.
1850 Cresy Report on sanitary conditions of Battle.
1852 S.E. Railway station opened at Battle and line to Hastings. Board of Health commenced following Cresy Report. In 1884 this became Battle U.D.C.; 1933 Battle R.D.C.; 1974 combined with Bexhill-on-Sea, Rye, and surrounding area to form Rother District Council.
1859 Battle Drill Hall built.
1861 Battle Police Station built.
1862 Cemetery opened.
1866 Battle churchyard closed for burials.
1867 Abbey Lodge of Freemasons opened.
1876 Closure of the gunpowder manufactory.
1890–1896 (between). Severe winters. Special train ran from Hastings with skaters for Powdermill Pond.
1900 Waterworks at Powdermill Lane opened. The one at Whatlington Road could only supply water three times a week to the town, and during a drought, twice a week. The supply came from wells and two springs.
1903–4 Market Green metalled.
1929 King George V came to Battle Abbey.
1935 Queen Mary visited Battle Abbey. King George VI and Queen Elizabeth visited town.
1966 Visit of Her Majesty Queen Elizabeth II and Prince Philip to the Abbey, town and St Mary's church.

TABLE OF POPULATION OF BATTLE PARISH. (8,252 acres)

c. 1400	abt. 1,000	1861	3,293	1931	3,491
1801	2,040	1871	3,495	1941	N/A
1811	2,531	1881	3,319	1951	4,300
1821	2,852	1891	3,153	1961	4,517
1831	2,999	1901	2,996	1971	4,987
1841	3,039	1911	2,924	1981	5,056
1851	3,849	1921	2,891		

(From *Victoria County History of Sussex*, p. 222)

It is thought that the population for 1851 was higher than average, due to an influx of labour working on the railway in the area.